Kunce

DISCARD

D1482213

Kranz

A New True Book

THE SUPREME COURT

By Carol Greene

CHILDRENS PRESS ™
CHICAGO

Aerial view of the Supreme Court

PHOTO CREDITS
Ankers Capitol Photographers—38
(2 photos), 39 (3 photos)
Gartman Agency/Photri—15, 17, 21, 23, 26, 29
The White House-Mary Anne Fackelman—30
Hillstrom Stock Photo:
© Milt and Joan Mann—Cover, 4, 10, 13 (2 photos), 45
© Brooks and Vankirk—11 (bottom)
Historical Pictures Service, Chicago—2, 7, 14, 18 (2 photos), 19, 20, 22, 42
Nawrocki Stock Photo:
© Jeff Apoian—11 (top)
© Larry Brooks—43
Roloc Color Slides—37 (2 photos), 40, 44
Charts by Horizon Graphics—6, 9, 33, 34
Cover: Supreme Court

Library of Congress Cataloging in Publication Data

Greene, Carol.
    The Supreme Court.

    (A New true book)
    Includes index
    Summary: Describes the function and structure of the
Supreme Court and gives a brief overview of some important
cases and well-known justices.
    1. United States. Supreme Court—Juvenile literature.
[1. United States. Supreme Court] I. Title.
KF8742.Z9G73   1985   347.73′26   84-23230
ISBN 0-516-01943-0   347.30735

TABLE OF CONTENTS

The Supreme Court is the highest court in the United States.

THE SUPREME COURT AND THE CONSTITUTION

The Supreme Court is the highest court in the United States. The job of the Supreme Court is to explain laws.

Some of these laws are in the United States Constitution. They are the most important laws in the country. They tell about people's rights and what people are free to do.

No other laws may disagree with the laws in the Constitution. If they do, the Supreme Court can say they are unconstitutional. Then they no longer are laws.

No laws passed by local, state, or federal governments can disagree with the Constitution of the United States.

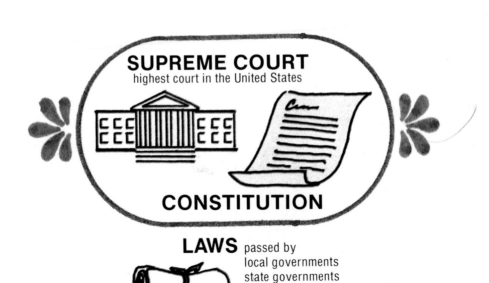

SUPREME COURT
highest court in the United States

CONSTITUTION

LAWS passed by
local governments
state governments
federal governments

Engraving of the Supreme Court made in 1888. From left to right: Associate Justices Lucias Lamar, Horace Gray, Joseph Bradley, Samuel Miller, Chief Justice Morrison Waite, Associate Justices Stephen Field, John Harlan, Stanley Matthews, Samuel Blatchford. Morrison R. Waite served as chief justice of the Supreme Court from 1874 to 1888.

Sometimes people have trouble understanding what a law in the Constitution means. Then the Supreme Court must explain, or interpret, this law.

THE SUPREME COURT AND THE U.S. GOVERNMENT

The Constitution divides the U.S. government into three branches. The Supreme Court is one of these branches. It is called the judicial branch.

The Senate and the House of Representatives are the legislative branch. They are also called

THREE BRANCHES OF GOVERNMENT

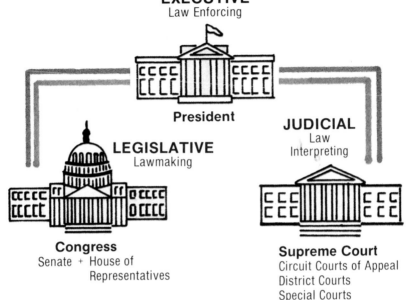

EXECUTIVE
Law Enforcing

President

LEGISLATIVE
Lawmaking

JUDICIAL
Law Interpreting

Congress
Senate + House of Representatives

Supreme Court
Circuit Courts of Appeal
District Courts
Special Courts

Congress. Their job is to make laws.

The president and the people who work for the president are the executive branch. Their job is to see that the laws are carried out.

The Constitution says each branch must do only its own job. That way no branch has too much power. This balance of power makes sure that one part of government never gets strong enough to overpower any other part.

The Supreme Court is the law-interpreting branch of the government.

The president of the United States lives and works in the White House. The president makes sure that the laws of the United States are enforced.

The House of Representatives and the Senate work in the Capitol. They make the laws for the United States.

THE SUPREME COURT AND THE STATES

Congress makes laws for the whole country. But the different states can make their own laws, too.

Sometimes a law made by Congress disagrees with a law made by a state. The Supreme Court must listen to both sides. Then it must decide which law is better. It must decide which law is right according to the Constitution.

Two statues, *Guardian of Law* (left) and *Contemplation of Justice* (right), stand in front of the Supreme Court.

Sometimes states make laws that disagree with the U.S. Constitution.

Suppose California made a law that no one in California could march in public to support a political cause.

In order to win the right to vote, American women marched in parades. They exercised their constitutional right to meet publicly to fight for their rights. The Nineteenth Amendment, passed in 1920, granted women the right to vote.

The Supreme Court would throw that law out. The Constitution says that people in the United States have the right to publicly meet and talk about anything they want. So California's law would be unconstitutional.

In the 1980s women marched trying to get the Equal Rights Amendment passed by state legislatures. Their political effort failed. Not enough states supported this amendment to make it a law.

Nothing can disagree with the U.S. Constitution. The president can't. The Congress can't. And the states can't. It is the job of the Supreme Court to make sure they don't.

THE SUPREME COURT JUSTICES

There are nine judges on the Supreme Court. They are called justices. Eight are associate justices. One is the chief justice. The chief justice does extra work to help run the court.

There are nine justices of the Supreme Court, from left to right, Associate Justices Thurgood Marshall, John P. Stevens, William J. Brennan, Lewis F. Powell, Chief Justice Warren E. Burger, Associate Justices William H. Rehnquist, Byron R. White, Sandra Day O'Connor, Harry A. Blackmun. The chief justice earns $100,700 a year. Associate justices receive $96,700.

In 1789 the Supreme Court met at the Royal Exchange (above) in New York City. The present Supreme Court (right) was built in the 1930s in Washington, D.C.

Congress decides how many justices there should be. The first Supreme Court had six. Then there were nine, then ten, then seven. But there have been nine now since 1869.

Justices serve on the Supreme Court until they die or retire. A justice can be removed by the other justices if he or she does something wrong. But it has never happened.

Oliver Wendell Holmes, Jr. served as a member of the Supreme Court of the United States from 1902 to 1932. Holmes believed that the law should develop and change to meet the changing needs of the people it was designed to safeguard.

Samuel Chase served as associate justice of the Supreme Court from 1796 to 1811. President George Washington appointed Chase to the Court.

Other justices did try to impeach one of the first justices, Samuel Chase. They said he had a bad temper. But that wasn't really a crime, so Chase stayed.

When a justice dies or retires, the president chooses a new one. That person's name goes to the Senate. The senators study the person carefully. If they think he or she will make a good justice, they vote yes.

At a hearing the senators question the individual the president has selected to fill a vacancy on the Supreme Court. The Senate must approve the president's choice.

Thurgood Marshall

In 1967, President Lyndon Johnson chose Thurgood Marshall to be on the Supreme Court. He was the first black person on the Court.

Sandra Day O'Connor with
President Ronald Reagan

Until 1981, all Supreme
Court justices were men.
People called them "The
Brethren." (That means
brothers.)

Then President Ronald
Reagan chose Sandra Day
O'Connor. She became the
first woman justice.

It is a great honor to be a Supreme Court justice. Most are trained as lawyers. Many have worked as judges in other courts.

But Supreme Court justices don't have to be judges or lawyers. Any U.S. citizen can be a Supreme Court justice—if the president chooses and the Senate approves.

U.S. Supreme Court Justices

Name	Term	Appointed By	Name	Term	Appointed By
Chief Justices			John M. Harlan	1877-1911	Hayes
John Jay	1790-1795	Washington	William B. Woods	1881-1887	Hayes
John Rutledge	1795	Washington	Stanley Matthews	1881-1889	Garfield
Oliver Ellsworth	1796-1800	Washington	Horace Gray	1882-1902	Arthur
John Marshall	1801-1835	J. Adams	Samuel Blatchford	1882-1893	Arthur
Roger B. Taney	1836-1864	Jackson	Lucius Q. C. Lamar	1888-1893	Cleveland
Salmon P. Chase	1864-1873	Lincoln	David J. Brewer	1890-1910	Harrison
Morrison R. Waite	1874-1888	Grant	Henry B. Brown	1891-1906	Harrison
Melville W. Fuller	1888-1910	Cleveland	George Shiras, Jr.	1892-1903	Harrison
Edward D. White	1910-1921	Taft	Howell E. Jackson	1893-1895	Harrison
William H. Taft	1921-1930	Harding	Edward D. White	1894-1910	Cleveland
Charles E. Hughes	1930-1941	Hoover	Rufus W. Peckham	1896-1909	Cleveland
Harlan F. Stone	1941-1946	F. D. Roosevelt	Joseph McKenna	1898-1925	McKinley
Frederick M. Vinson	1946-1953	Truman	Oliver W. Holmes, Jr.	1902-1932	T. Roosevelt
Earl Warren	1953-1969	Eisenhower	William R. Day	1903-1922	T. Roosevelt
Warren E. Burger	1969-	Nixon	William H. Moody	1906-1910	T. Roosevelt
			Horace H. Lurton	1910-1914	Taft
Associate Justices			Charles E. Hughes	1910-1916	Taft
James Wilson	1789-1798	Washington	Willis Van Devanter	1911-1937	Taft
John Rutledge	1790-1791	Washington	Joseph R. Lamar	1911-1916	Taft
William Cushing	1790-1810	Washington	Mahlon Pitney	1912-1922	Taft
John Blair	1790-1796	Washington	James C. McReynolds	1914-1941	Wilson
James Iredell	1790-1799	Washington	Louis D. Brandeis	1916-1939	Wilson
Thomas Johnson	1792-1793	Washington	John H. Clarke	1916-1922	Wilson
William Paterson	1793-1806	Washington	George Sutherland	1922-1938	Harding
Samuel Chase	1796-1811	Washington	Pierce Butler	1923-1939	Harding
Bushrod Washington	1799-1829	J. Adams	Edward T. Sanford	1923-1930	Harding
Alfred Moore	1800-1804	J. Adams	Harlan F. Stone	1925-1941	Coolidge
Willam Johnson	1804-1834	Jefferson	Owen J. Roberts	1930-1945	Hoover
H. Brockholst Livingston	1807-1823	Jefferson	Benjamin N. Cardozo	1932-1938	Hoover
Thomas Todd	1807-1826	Jefferson	Hugo L. Black	1937-1971	F. D. Roosevelt
Gabriel Duvall	1811-1835	Madison	Stanley F. Reed	1938-1957	F. D. Roosevelt
Joseph Story	1812-1845	Madison	Felix Frankfurter	1939-1962	F. D. Roosevelt
Smith Thompson	1823-1843	Monroe	William O. Douglas	1939-1975	F. D. Roosevelt
Robert Trimble	1826-1828	J. Q. Adams	Frank Murphy	1940-1949	F. D. Roosevelt
John McLean	1830-1861	Jackson	James F. Byrnes	1941-1942	F. D. Roosevelt
Henry Baldwin	1830-1844	Jackson	Robert H. Jackson	1941-1954	F. D. Roosevelt
James M. Wayne	1835-1867	Jackson	Wiley B. Rutledge	1943-1949	F. D. Roosevelt
Philip P. Barbour	1836-1841	Jackson	Harold H. Burton	1945-1958	Truman
John Catron	1837-1865	Van Buren	Tom C. Clark	1949-1967	Truman
John McKinley	1838-1852	Van Buren	Sherman Minton	1949-1956	Truman
Peter V. Daniel	1842-1860	Van Buren	John M. Harlan	1955-1971	Eisenhower
Samuel Nelson	1845-1872	Tyler	William J. Brennan, Jr.	1956-	Eisenhower
Levi Woodbury	1845-1851	Polk	Charles E. Whittaker	1957-1962	Eisenhower
Robert C. Grier	1846-1870	Polk	Potter Stewart	1958-1981	Eisenhower
Benjamin R. Curtis	1851-1857	Fillmore	Byron R. White	1962-	Kennedy
John A. Campbell	1853-1861	Pierce	Arthur J. Goldberg	1962-1965	Kennedy
Nathan Clifford	1858-1881	Buchanan	Abe Fortas	1965-1969	Johnson
Noah H. Swayne	1862-1881	Lincoln	Thurgood Marshall	1967-	Johnson
Samuel F. Miller	1862-1890	Lincoln	Harry A. Blackmun	1970-	Nixon
David Davis	1862-1877	Lincoln	Lewis F. Powell, Jr.	1972-	Nixon
Stephen J. Field	1863-1897	Lincoln	William H. Rehnquist, Jr.	1972-	Nixon
William Strong	1870-1880	Grant	John P. Stevens	1975-	Ford
Joseph P. Bradley	1870-1892	Grant	Sandra Day O'Connor	1981-	Reagan
Ward Hunt	1873-1882	Grant			

The words "Equal Justice Under Law" are carved into the marble above the entrance to the Supreme Court.

THE SUPREME COURT AT WORK

The Supreme Court works in a beautiful white marble building in Washington, D.C. Across the front are carved the words "Equal Justice Under Law." This means the Supreme Court does not play favorites—with anyone.

The Court begins work on the first Monday in October. This work time is called a term. It lasts until May, June, or later.

Around fifteen hundred cases come before the Supreme Court each term. It can hear only about two hundred of them. All the justices decide which cases they will hear.

Interior of the Supreme Court. The nine justices sit behind the bench when they hear cases.

They listen to cases in a special courtroom. There is no jury. There are no witnesses. Lawyers tell both sides. The justices ask them questions.

Warren E. Burger was appointed chief justice by President Richard Nixon in 1969.

Then the justices meet to talk about the cases they have heard. They vote on a decision for each case. At least five justices must agree. The chief justice can write a report of the Court's decision or ask one of the other justices to do it.

All the justices look at the report. They make sure it says exactly what they mean. Justices who do not agree can write their own reports. These are called dissenting opinions.

Then the decisions are read in court. Newspapers print them. The official version goes into the Supreme Court record. And everyone knows what those laws mean now.

HOW THE COURTS WORK

Not all cases go to the Supreme Court. The Supreme Court hears only cases about federal laws or the Constitution. Other cases must go to other courts.

Suppose a man stole some money. He was caught and his case went to a trial court. He had a lawyer to defend him. Still the jury found him guilty.

He could appeal that guilty verdict to a higher

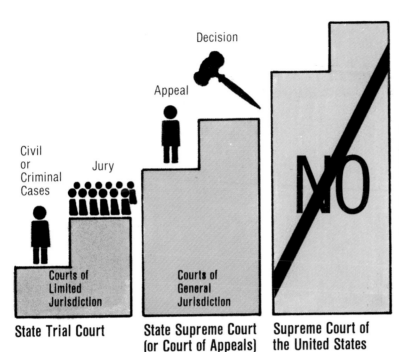

Decision

Appeal

Civil
or
Criminal
Cases

Jury

Courts of
Limited
Jurisdiction

State Trial Court

Courts of
General
Jurisdiction

**State Supreme Court
(or Court of Appeals)**

NO

**Supreme Court of
the United States**

Most civil and
criminal cases are
handled by state courts.
Every state in the
United States also has
its own state supreme
court, or court
of appeals.

state court. But he could
not take it to the Supreme
Court. It is not about a
federal law or the
Constitution. None of his
rights under the Constitution
had been denied him at his
jury trial.

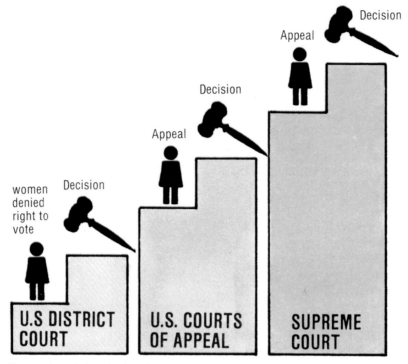

women denied right to vote

Decision

Appeal

Decision

Appeal

Decision

U.S DISTRICT COURT

U.S. COURTS OF APPEAL

SUPREME COURT

Cases involving federal law or the Constitution first are heard in lower, or district, courts.

But suppose a city passed a law that said women could not vote in city elections. A group of women felt this law was unconstitutional. The

Constitution says women
can vote, just as men can.

These women might start
at a United States district
court. Then they might go
on to a federal court of
appeals. They might even
end up at the Supreme
Court.

The Supreme Court
could hear this case. It is
about the Constitution.
(And the women would
win. Do you know why?)

FAMOUS JUSTICES

Some great people have served on the Supreme Court. They have done much to shape U.S. history.

John Jay was the first chief justice. He worked on a treaty to end bad feelings between the U.S. and England after the revolutionary war.

John Jay (left) was chief justice of the Supreme Court from 1790 to 1795. He was appointed by President George Washington. John Marshall (right) served on the Supreme Court from 1801 to 1835. He was appointed by President John Adams.

John Marshall became chief justice in 1801. He showed that the Supreme Court could throw out Congress's laws if they went against the Constitution.

Charles Evans Hughes (left) was chief justice from 1930 to 1941. He was appointed by President Herbert Hoover. Oliver Wendell Holmes (right) was appointed associate justice by President Theodore Roosevelt.

Oliver Wendell Holmes joined the Supreme Court in 1902. He often disagreed with other justices. Holmes thought that people's needs changed. So laws should change, too. He wrote a book called *The Common Law.*

Louis D. Brandeis (top left) was
appointed to the Court by President
Woodrow Wilson. He served from 1916
to 1939. In 1921 President Warren G. Harding
appointed William H. Taft (above) chief
justice of the Supreme Court. Taft
served until 1930. Earl Warren (below
left) was appointed chief justice by
President Dwight D. Eisenhower in 1953.
He served on the court until 1969.

Some other great
justices have been Charles
Evans Hughes, Louis
Brandeis, William H. Taft,
and Earl Warren.

Main hall of the Supreme Court.

FAMOUS CASES

Supreme Court decisions have made many changes in life in the United States. In the Scottsboro Nine case, justices said that people on trial have the right to a lawyer. They also

An attorney meets with the young men identified as the Scottsboro Nine.

said that black people must be allowed to serve on juries.

In the Linda Brown case, the justices said that black children and white children should not go to separate schools.

The Supreme Court decision in the Linda Brown case led to integration in classrooms throughout the United States.

Before the Gerald Gault case, children in juvenile courts did not have the same rights as adults. Then the justices said that children must be protected by the Constitution, too.

The seal of the Supreme Court appears on all official documents.

These are only a few famous cases heard by the Supreme Court. There have been many others. And there will be many more as the Supreme Court goes on doing its very important job.

WORDS YOU SHOULD KNOW

associates(ah • SOH • see • its) — persons closely connected for common purpose

branch(BRANCH) — a division or part of something

case(KAYSS) — a suit or some other action in law

court(KORT) — a judge or several judges meeting to hear law cases

dissenting opinion(dis • ENT • ing oh • PIN • yun) — a justice's different opinion that does not agree with the majority of justices on the court

executive(egg • ZEK • yoo • tiv) — the branch of government that sees that laws are carried out and that the government runs smoothly

federal(FED • er • al) — a type of central govenment formed by units; the individual units keep some powers, but give most of them to the central government

impeach(im • PEECH) — to charge a public governmental official with wrongdoing

judge(JUHJ) — a governmental official who has the power to decide cases brought before a court of law

judicial(joo • DISH • il) — the branch of government that tries cases brought before it and issues opinions and makes decisions regarding the law

jury(JOO • ree) — a group of people who listen to evidence and give a verdict regarding a case in court

justice(JUSS • tiss) — the principle of being fair and just under the law; also, a name for the judges who serve on high courts

juvenile court(JOO • vih • nyl KORT) — a court that hears cases involving young persons, usually under eighteen years old

laws(LAWZ) — rules or orders that must be obeyed or observed

lawyer(LAW • yer) — a person whose job is to help and advise people about the law and work for them in courts

legislative(lej • iss • LAY • tiv) — the branch of government that makes laws

opinion(oh • PIN • yun) — a written explanation, by a judge or justice, about a legal decision

rights(RITES) — the powers and privileges under law to which people are entitled

term(TURM) — the time during which something lasts; in legal terms, the time when a court is in session

treaty(TREET • ee) — a written agreement between two or more nations

unconstitutional(un • kon • stih • TOOSH • in • il) — not according to the facts as set down in a constitution

witnesses(WIT • ness • ez) — people who testify about their knowledge of something in a court of law

INDEX

About the author

Carol Greene has degrees in English literature and musicology. She has worked in international exchange programs as an editor and as a teacher. She now lives in St. Louis, Missouri, and writes full-time. She has had published over fifty books—most of them for children. Other Childrens Press books by Ms. Greene include England, Japan, Poland, *and* Yugoslavia *(in the Enchantment of the World series);* Marie Curie *and* Louisa May Alcott *(in the People of Distinction series);* Holidays Around the World, Robots, Music, Language, The United Nations, Astronauts, Presidents, *and* Congress *(in the True Book series);* The Thirteen Days of Halloween; A Computer Went A-Courting; *and* Sandra Day O'Connor: First Woman on the Supreme Court.